KU-437-572

Contents

It's spring!

How do you know

it's spring?

Spring is full of life.

Pebble® Plus

Investigate the Seasons

Let's Look at Spring

Revised Edition

Sarah L Schuette

Raintree is an imprint of Capstone Global Library Limited, a company incorporated in England and Wales having its registered office at 264 Banbury Road, Oxford, OX2 7DY – Registered company number: 6695582

www.raintree.co.uk
myorders@raintree.co.uk

Editorial credits
Sarah Bennett, designer; Tracy Cummins, media researcher, Laura Manthe, production specialist

Photo credits
Capstone Studio: Karon Dubke, 15; Shutterstock: Catalin Petolea, 21, Dmitry Strizhakov, 17, fotohunter, 9, Liubou Yasiukovich, Cover Design Element, Mariola Anna S, 7, Pakhnyushchy, 1, PCHT, Cover, RaJi, 13, shahreen, 11, StripedNadin, 3, Sunny Forest, 19, WH CHOW, 5

Printed and bound in India.

ISBN 978 1 4747 5659 4 (hardback)
22 21 20 19 18
10 9 8 7 6 5 4 3 2 1

ISBN 978 1 4747 5664 8 (paperback)
23 22 21 20 19
10 9 8 7 6 5 4 3 2 1

British Library Cataloguing in Publication Data
A full catalogue record for this book is available from the British Library.

Bright sunlight shines.

The next day rain falls.

Spring days are warmer
and wetter than winter days.

Sun and rain help

plants grow.

Everything is green again.

Animals in spring

What happens
to animals in spring?
Birds feed their young
in nests.

11

Sheep graze

in green pastures.

Newborn lambs walk

on wobbly legs.

Plants in spring

What happens to plants

in spring?

Tulips bloom.

Grass grows.

Blossoms cover cherry trees.

Bees buzz in and out

of the flowers.

Planting begins on farms.

Rows of crops

sprout in fields.

What's next?

The weather gets warmer.

Spring is over.

What season comes next?

Glossary

blossom flower on a fruit tree or other plant

crop plant grown in large amounts; corn, wheat, soybeans and oats are some crops planted in spring

graze eat grass that is growing in a field

pasture field of grass where animals graze

season one of the four parts of the year; winter, spring, summer and autumn are seasons

sprout start to grow

wobbly unsteady

Find out more

Books

Spring (Seasons), Stephanie Turnbull (Franklin Watts, 2015)

The Seasons (Our Special World), Liz Lennon (Franklin Watts, 2016)

What Can You See in Spring? (Seasons), Sian Smith (Raintree, 2014)

Websites

www.woodlandtrust.org.uk/naturedetectives/activities/2016/03/
spring-hunt Go on a spring hunt with the Woodlands Trust.

www.dkfindout.com/uk/earth/seasons
Find out more about the seasons on this website.

Comprehension questions

1. What helps plants grow?

2. Describe two signs that it is spring.

3. How is spring different from winter?

Index